The Countryside Code

Be safe - plan ahead and follow any signs

Leave gates and property as you find them

Protect plants and animals, and take your litter home

Keep dogs under close control

Consider other people

Walking is a healthy pursuit in the open air. Medical advice suggests we can all benefit from gentle exercise in terms of improved circulation and respiration and as an aid to maintaining our general fitness.

Let's get walking!

Breckland Walks

Twelve circular walks in Breckland

SIMON MALONE

Larks Press

Published by the Larks Press
Ordnance Farmhouse, Guist Bottom, Dereham,
Norfolk NR20 5PF
01328 829207
Larks.Press@btinternet.com
Website: www.booksatlarkspress.co.uk

Printed by the Lanceni Press,
Garrood Drive, Fakenham, Norfolk

2006

British Library Cataloguing–in-Publication Data
A catalogue record for this book is available
from the British Library

For Megan, my Granddaughter,
born March 2005

Acknowledgements: *Thanks to the Culford Village Hall Management Committee for permission to use their car park, and to the Norfolk Museums Archaeology Service and the Highways Departments of Norfolk and Suffolk County Councils for their guidance and advice.*

ISBN 1 904006 31 0

Twelve Circular Walks in the Brecks

by Simon Malone

This little book will allow you to explore the interesting and unique Brecks countryside easily on foot. It is a companion to my earlier book *Thetford Forest Walks* and this time most of the walks are wholly in the open Brecks countryside. Compared to some other parts of England, the Brecks are sparsely served with public rights of way. This probably results from relatively small populations of people living here in the past, combined with the effect of earlier land being in the ownership of a relatively small number of large country estates. I have put together what I hope you will find are interesting circular walks, avoiding the use of busy public roads as much as possible and at the same time trying to keep clear of routes that pass through Thetford Forest, the subject of a number of walks in my earlier book. Nevertheless, some of the walks do pass through short sections of the Forest, such is its significance across the Brecks.

In the main the walks follow public footpaths, bridlepaths and by-ways with occasional usage of roads, lanes or permissive paths for short distances.

The walks vary in length, ranging from 4-mile walks, which are enjoyable for the family, to more strenuous 8-mile walks. Some walks have the option of being shortened if necessary.

All the walks start at easily located places where cars may be parked easily. For security reasons it is sensible to remove all valuable items from your car before you start.

Please follow the Countryside Code at all times and, in particular, observe any warning signs.

I hope you will enjoy your exploration of the sandy Brecks, one of England's unique and distinctive areas.

The Walks

Ordnance Survey Explorer Series 1:25000 scale maps covering the routes described in this booklet are: No. 226 'Ely and Newmarket', No. 229 'Thetford Forest in the Brecks', No. 230 'Diss and Harleston' and No. 236 'Kings Lynn, Downham Market and Swaffham'

Disclaimer: *Walkers use the routes described in this booklet at their own risk. The routes of the walks use various categories of public rights of way and the information is correct at the time of going to press. However, such routes may be subject to change and may not always be clearly defined on the ground. The author cannot accept any responsibility for this. If in any doubt, walkers should check with their local county highways department before starting any walk.*

The Brecks – Land of Flint and Sand

Breckland, or the Brecks as it is commonly called, is an extensive region of some 370 square miles straddling the Norfolk-Suffolk border, which is characterised by light sandy soil, areas of heathland and a field pattern hedged by ancient and gnarled Scots pine trees, the like of which is not to be found elsewhere in England.

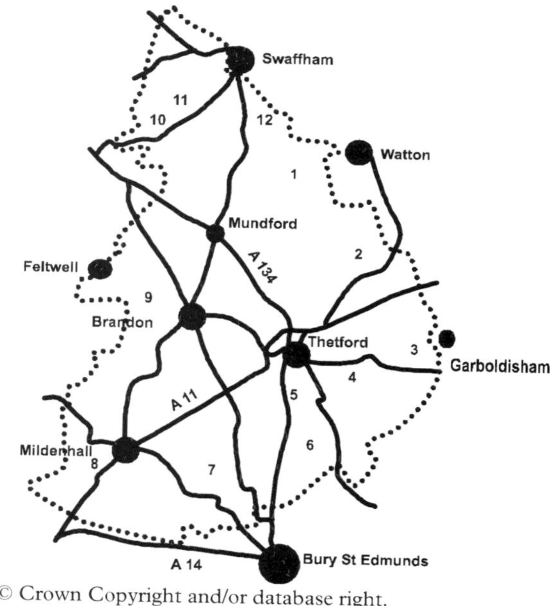

There is no precisely defined physical boundary to this region, but most authorities regard it as stretching more or less from Bury St Edmunds towards Mildenhall in the south, and Swaffham and across to Watton in the north, bounded by the Fens to the west and reaching towards East Harling and Garboldisham in the east. It is roughly within this area that the light, sandy soils characteristic of the Brecks are at their most widespread; though even within this area there are some parts where heavier soils with ponds and meres exist.

The Brecks and the locations of the walks

In past centuries these light and generally sandy soils, situated in one of the driest regions of the entire British Isles, had relatively little agricultural value. Indeed their main use was to graze sheep and, in the Middle Ages, to provide extensive rabbit warrens, where rabbits were farmed for their meat and their fur.

The result of this type of continuous land use, with overgrazing by animals, was a landscape notable for its sparse vegetation. Limited cultivation of crops took place, mostly quite transient as farmers used up any natural fertility in the soil and moved on to 'break' new ground.

Hence 'break' became Breck and the famous Thetford historian and naturalist W. G. Clarke coined the name 'Breckland' in 1894.

The sandy soils were deposited by wind and melt-water as the ice sheets retreated after the last Ice Age and they vary in depth over the underlying chalk bedrock. Where they are of some depth they are acid in nature with heather, gorse and other heath plants dominant. The shallower soils are variably more alkaline and their flora is totally different. In some areas this soil variation occurs as patterns in the soil, (sometimes as irregular stripes), which are the result of permafrost activity associated with the last Ice Age. In such situations the different plant communities co-exist side by side. It is this heath and soil/plant ecology that makes the Brecks such a wonderful area for plant and animal communities, many plants, in particular, being unique to this part of the British Isles. Stone curlew, woodlark and nightjar, all of which are protected, scarce birds, either nationally or internationally, have always been present in the Brecks and thanks to the positive actions of foresters, farmers and the various wildlife agencies their numbers have increased significantly in recent years.

Because of the sandy nature of the soils, the scarcity of vegetation and the low rainfall, the area was always prone to blowing sand and in some places dunes were a feature in past centuries. The Little Ouse River at Santon Downham was partially blocked by blown sand in 1668 and the village virtually swamped by the sand. In order to stabilise the soil and begin the process of improving the land for growing agricultural crops, hedges, mainly of Scots pine, were planted in the late 18th and 19th centuries. The hedges became known as 'deal rows', deal being the name for sawn pine timber. The Elveden Estate, near Thetford, was a major pioneer of a number of methods of bringing the inhospitable Brecks into valuable agricultural use.

Scots pine is a forest tree by nature but can be developed into a hedge by trimming new growth in the spring and for a long period these hedges were maintained in this way, affording shelter to the soil and reducing devastating blows. However, as the sandy wastes were brought under control and labour costs rose together with labour shortages during The Great War, the practice of trimming these hedges each year fell into neglect. The Scots pine hedges began to revert to lines of closely planted trees resulting in the gnarled and contorted pine trees we see today which characterise the field boundary system unique to the Brecks.

At the beginning of the 20th century agriculture was in the midst of depression. The few large estates in the area were in financial difficulties. At the same time, the country had endured the Great War of 1914-18 and the government of the day was counting the cost to British woodlands. These had been stripped to provide timber for the war effort, requiring vast quantities of timber for the coal mines and industry at home and for the construction of trenches and fortifications in France. At the same time German naval blockades had prevented vital timber imports from reaching us in sufficient quantities. As a result the Forestry Commission came into being in 1919 and early acquisitions to its estate were made in the Brecks which accounts for the Thetford Forest we know today. A large part of the central Brecks is also used as a training area by the military authorities and although, sadly, this is lost to public access, it is now of significant importance for its wildlife conservation value.

Nowadays, modern agriculture has completed the process of taming this inhospitable environment completely and, thanks largely to irrigation and the use of modern fertilisers, very valuable arable crops can be grown including carrots, parsnips, onions, lettuce, potatoes and sugar beet, as well as all the usual cereal crops.

1. Merton and Thompson

Grid reference of start TL 907988 *Distance 6 miles*

This walk starts from the green in the village of Merton. This tiny village is located on the A1075 road between Watton and Thetford. Half a mile or so south of Watton take the B1110 signed Merton and Thompson. Drive south on this road for about a mile turning right at the crossroads to arrive at the green which is surrounded by picturesque cottages and contains the pretty village shelter described later. Refreshments on the walk may be obtained from the Chequers Inn at Thompson.

The Walk

Park your car on the edge of the green, which is surrounded by tiny roads and walk back the way you drove a short distance, looking for a signed footpath on your right leading down a shingle drive between houses. Very soon you will see a plaque confirming you are on the footpath, known locally as Sally's Walk, which leads away from the shingled drive as a grass path with a conifer hedge on your right. Initially this is a well mown path leading past the corner of a garden and along a field and then as a hedged path leading into a wood.

When you reach a stony road, turn left and follow this until you reach a white gate through which you arrive at a main road. Just before this point the **Merton Parish Church of Saint Peter** is across a small green to your right. A short deviation takes you to the church and there is a fine view of Merton Park and Merton Hall from the high ground at the rear of the church.

Passing through the white gate, turn right and follow the main road.

This is by no means busy but you are sure to encounter a few cars. After about a quarter of a mile, turn right at a T-junction with the war memorial for the village of Tottington on the corner opposite. This leads into a very quiet lane, the first of several you will encounter on this walk, which now leads only to the boundary of a large military training area some distance ahead. This was once an access road to Tottington village, which, along with several other villages and some seventeen thousand acres of land, was commandeered by the military authorities during the Second World War.

Follow this lane for about a quarter of a mile until, opposite a roadside cottage, you see the footpath signed on your left. Cross a stile and follow the track along the edge of a small clearing with a wood on your left. The path is well defined across another grass field, jinking through a fence and following the fence on your left before going gently downhill through a wood. This section of the path is also well defined but may be somewhat overtopped by vegetation in high summer. At the bottom of the wood, pass a stile and the path bears hard left, crosses over another grassy track and continues straight ahead, becoming a path between hedges and then emerging as a short length of path across a garden lawn and leading out into a quiet lane lined with houses and cottages.

In due course this brings you out onto the junction of Watton Road and Mill Lane in the village of Thompson. At this point our walk turns right into Marlpit Lane, another 'no through road' due to the military training area. However, if you want to visit the picturesque local pub, The Chequers Inn, go straight along Mill Lane for about two hundred yards and turn left into Griston Road. You will find the pub a short

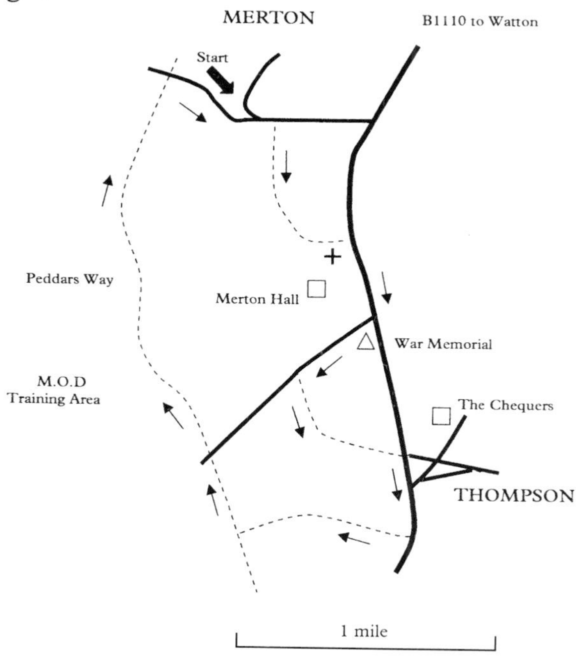

distance along on the left. Good beers and pub food are available at the appropriate times of day. Return to Marlpit Lane and continue the walk.

A short distance down Marlpit Lane you will pass a converted barn on your right and the road bears right into Tottington Road. Follow this, keeping to the tarmac road and ignoring the stony road leading straight ahead at a right hand bend. Eventually the tarmac road is blocked by the gated entry to the training area. Here you turn right onto the Peddars Way, a long-distance national trail, and follow this for a considerable distance as it follows the fenced boundary of the training area. For much of this section the path is narrow, generally with woods and fields on either side. It crosses another tarmac road and continues straight ahead passing a marker stone with a quotation about surveyors carved on it. Shortly after this, the trail passes through gates and moves away from the military area to cross wooded farmland. The narrow path becomes a stony track passing a house on the left and for a short section is a tarmac drive past a house on the right. It leads through an avenue of oak trees with Home Farm on your left and barns on the right.

At a crossroads the Peddars Way goes hard left and you turn hard right onto a tarmac lane which soon leads you back to the green at Merton.

Did you know that....

The pretty thatched flint shelter standing near a corner of the green at Merton was built by the village to commemorate the silver jubilee of Queen Elizabeth in June 1977. It makes a perfect spot to rest at the end of the walk and perhaps to eat a picnic.

The Chequers Inn is a quintessentially English country pub. Built in the 16th century it boasts many original features, including exposed beams and a thatched roof which reaches low down close to head level. Manor courts were held here at least from 1724 and perhaps even earlier. It prides itself on the selection of real ales it offers and serves fine food in both the bars and the restaurant. With its Bed and Breakfast facilities it is well placed to offer overnight accommodation to ramblers intending to walk the complete length of the Peddars Way.

Saint Peter's church in its present form dates from the 14th century. The Norman tower contains three bells and the base of the tower, which was built in three stages, is believed to be Saxon. In 1885 Lord and Lady Walsingham of nearby Merton Hall erected a carved oak reredos as a memorial to the Reverend George Crabbe, rector of Merton for 34 years. In 1889 Lady Walsingham presented the church with a new organ. For more information about Merton village, visit the web site **www.merton.ukgo.com** which contains a wealth of information about the village and its locality.

The large military training area often referred to locally as the **Battle Area**, is used by the army to train troops for a wide range of modern warfare. The military authorities commandeered much of the area during the Second World War and a number of villages were evacuated completely. The area has remained in the jurisdiction of the army since then. Occasionally organised tours take place and give members of the public a chance to glimpse a little of the history of the area. Enquire at local libraries or Tourist Information Centres about such tours. As well as being a major training area the Battle Area is also renowned for its wildlife conservation, being one of the largest areas of Breckland heath remaining today.

2. East Wretham and Illington

Grid reference for start TL915906 *Distance 5 or 8 miles*

The walk starts from the church in the village of East Wretham, or simply Wretham as it is often called. From Thetford take the A1075 Watton road and after about four miles you will reach the tiny village of Wretham. Go straight over the crossroads, keeping to the main road, and look for Church Road on your left just before you reach the tower of a **windmill** which has been converted into a dwelling. Follow this lane until you reach the church and park in the car park provided next to it. There are no refreshment facilities on this walk, the local village pub having closed in recent years.

N.B. I have indicated on the map that it is possible to shorten the walk by returning to Stonebridge via the Peddars Way thus missing the loop through Illington. This shorter walk is 5 miles in length.

The Walk

Start the walk by going back the way you came away from the church and then turning right, passing Manor Farm on your left. Keep directly ahead to the crossroads and go straight over along a straight lane with army camps on either side. When you reach a main road again, cross straight over along a tarmac drive with a house and wooden outbuildings on the right. There is a finger post showing this to be a Public Path. Soon after you pass a further house on the left, the tarmac drive bears right and you go straight ahead along a grass path skirting a field on your left to enter Roudham Forest.

At this point the Public Path goes off to the left through the trees. However, it is poorly defined and in the summer may be overgrown. The alternative is to keep straight ahead on a good hard track. This is Forestry Commission land with open access to the public so using this alternative is permissible. After a couple of hundred yards you reach a more important forest road and here you turn left. This is the Harling Drove which is a public right of way. As the Drove passes the corner of a field you reach the point where the formal Public Path would have joined the Drove had you been able to walk it.

Keep straight ahead through the brick abutments of a demolished bridge which once carried the railway that ran from the main line at nearby Roudham Junction to Watton. Ignore any side turnings. The stony forest road forks and you take the right hand fork to reach another stony road with a small cottage off to your right. This cottage was once the home of the railway crossing keeper and his family. Turn left onto this stony road which, as well as being a forest road, is the route of the Peddars Way National Trail. You are at the eastern end of the Harling Drove at this point and it runs westward, mainly through Thetford Forest, to reach Weeting and Hockwold on the edge of the Fens some 13 miles away.

Keep to the Peddars Way as it climbs gently uphill, ignoring the forest road which goes off to the right. Just before you reach a large, and sometimes noisy, gas pumping station on the right, take the track to the right which skirts the forest edge with open fields on your left. ***(This is the point where you continue straight ahead along the Peddars Way if you choose the shorter walk).*** The track bears right around a corner of the wood and soon re-enters the forest on a wide grass ride with pine plantations either side. It goes gently downhill to reach a stony forest road with a field in front of you.

Turn left along this road, ignoring the signed bridle path to the right and when the stony road bears hard right continue straight ahead along a short stretch of hard chalky track to reach the forest boundary with an open field landscape in front of you. In the distance you will see traffic on the A11 Norwich road.

Turn left along the forest boundary with a steel radio mast on the corner and follow the track, which is variously sandy or grassy, along the edge of the fields. As you leave the forest behind, keep straight ahead, climbing gently uphill on a grassy path. As the path reaches the brow of the hill keep straight ahead to begin the gentle descent to the tiny hamlet of Illington with its church visible off to your right.

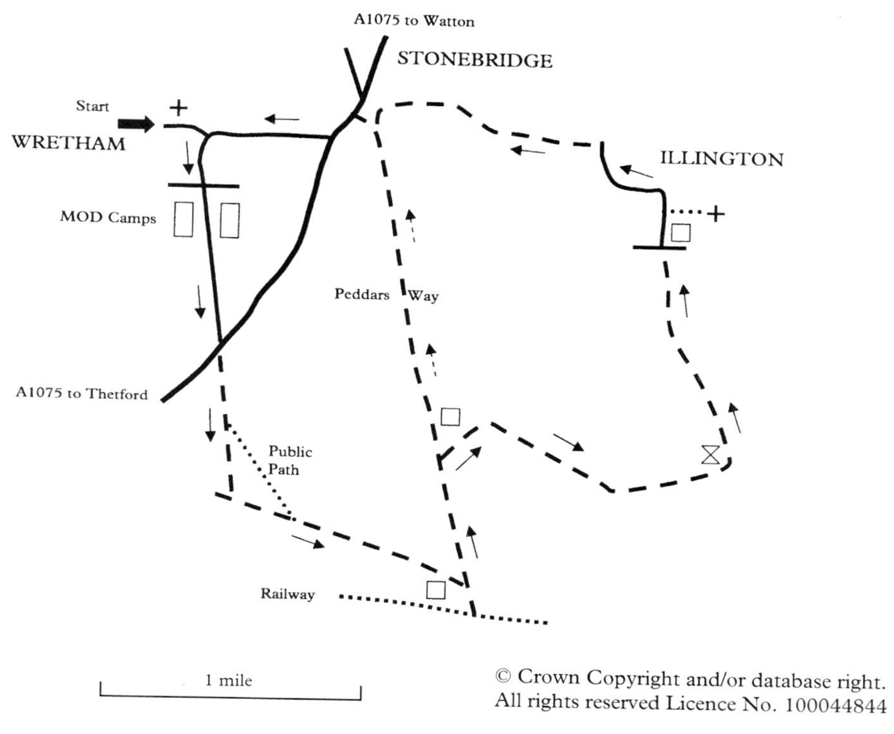

You will reach a public road at this point and need to go straight across down a very small lane signposted Illington Village with bungalows on the corner to your right. When you reach a barn on your right take the track through the steel gate between the barn and a bungalow to visit Illington church. The track is signed as a Bridle Path and only leads to the church which is a short distance away. Return to the tarmac lane and turn right to continue downhill.

Keep to the tarmac lane as it bears left, ignoring another footpath off to the right. This lane passes a number of cottages set back behind trees and shrubs on the right and then bears right to become a stony track between fields. Ignore the signed footpath off to the left as this is now closed and replaced by an Official Diversion. After a short distance the track reaches the corner of a wood.

At this point the Official Diversion, which is the route to take, is signed left to follow the southern bank of a small stream for about a mile. Simply follow the fence line along the stream edge on your right. You will go through a number of gates and for a lengthy stretch the path runs through scrubby grassland with cultivated land a hundred yards or more off to the left. The last gate takes you back into agricultural land with a house visible off to the right beyond the stream. Walk ahead to the corner of the field and turn left uphill for about a hundred and forty yards and go through a gate on the right. ***(You have now reached the Peddars Way where the shorter route will meet up if you have chosen to walk it.)*** Go straight ahead through the abutments of a demolished railway bridge. Bear right onto a tarmac drive between houses and gardens to reach a main road in the hamlet of Stonebridge.

Cross over and turn left along the pavement, (which is signposted as Cycle Route 13), and just after you pass the entrance to an abandoned army camp on your left, turn right into Church Lane, which you drove down originally on your way to the start of the walk. Follow Church Lane, passing Wretham Village Hall on your right, to go back to Wretham Church and its car park.

Did you know that....

The Harling Drove runs from Roudham Heath in the east through to Hockwold-cum-Wilton on the edge of the fens to the west. At one time it originated at East Harling, even further to the east, but that section of the route is untraceable having been largely lost by the construction of the railway and other developments in earlier centuries. It is a historic Drove road developed for the purpose of moving stock and other goods to and from the Fens and the Norfolk hinterland. For much of its distance it runs on sandy paths and tracks through the forest, although, after leaving the forest near Weeting, it now follows the line of modern roads.

The area has a long history of connection to the military, there having been a **World War 2 airfield** nearby which flew the Wellingtons and Lancasters of 311 and 115 squadrons. Also nearby is the large military training area, locally known as the **Battle Area**. The nearby army camps are still very much in use, although that at Stonebridge is now closed.

The **church of Saint Ethelbert**, **East Wretham** was rebuilt in 1865. Its parish register dates from 1748. The church is normally locked but details of local key holders are given in the church porch.

The **church of Saint Andrew, Illington**, is a flint building in the Perpendicular and Early English styles. The square tower contains three bells. The structure was fully restored in 1847. Today it sits lonely and isolated amongst farmland. It is locked and there is no indication of how access may be obtained.

Formerly **Wretham** comprised the hamlets of East and West Wretham. The latter is now mostly within the adjoining military training area and its church is a ruin. The hamlet of Stonebridge also lies within the parish of Wretham. The only pub in the locality, The Dog and Partridge in Stonebridge, is closed at the time of writing, (2005).

For an explanation of this village sign and many others see *Timpson on the Verge*, and *Timpson on the Verge 2*.

3. Garboldisham and the Devil's Ditch

Grid reference of start *TM 005816* *Distance 6 miles*

This walk starts from the village of Garboldisham, nine miles east of Thetford on the A1066 road. Turn left at the crossroads by The Fox Inn and immediately left into Church Street where you should be able to park safely. The village name is pronounced 'Garblesham'. **The Fox Inn**, which is at the village crossroads, serves food and drink at the usual opening hours and the village shop is on the south side of the A1066 road.

The Walk

Climb the steps at the start of the footpath immediately opposite the entrance to the church and follow this path between houses and then along the fenced edge of a small field. When you reach Water Lane turn right and descend the hill to the main road. Turn left here and, keeping to the verge for about 150 yards, follow the road until you see the next footpath on the right hand side.

Take this path going round the railings which prevent people from exiting the path onto the main road too quickly. Follow it uphill with a shelterbelt on your left. When you reach the T-junction with another path by a house, turn right and keep straight ahead to the next main road. Cross straight over by the bridleway finger post and follow this gravel track for about half a mile until you reach a small lane in the hamlet of Smallworth.

Turn right along the street and take the next lane left signposted to Blo Norton. This is a designated 'Quiet Lane', one of several in this area identified by Norfolk County Council as one where traffic use is intended to be minimised voluntarily. The Quiet Lane ends at a T-junction and you turn right, signposted Hopton. This lane in turn leads you to the B1111 where you turn left, signed Bury St Edmunds, quickly crossing the Little Ouse River to enter Suffolk. This is a slightly busier road but you are only on it for a quarter of a mile or so and the verge is wide enough to use to avoid traffic.

Turn right into Mill Lane, initially a concrete farm drive which in turn becomes a gravel farm track running straight ahead for some distance. A footpath joining from the left is the Angles Way which starts at the mouth of the River Yare in Great Yarmouth and at this point is nearing its end at Knettishall Heath a few miles ahead.

The gravel track becomes a grass track for a short distance and the path dog-legs off to the left, crosses a wooden footbridge and then sets off across fields with a fence line on your right. At the end of the fields the path goes right, crossing a wooden footbridge over the Little Ouse and back into Norfolk again. It then continues straight ahead aiming towards a group of steel farm silos in front. It passes close to the silos on your right and reaches a tarmac farm drive where you turn left.

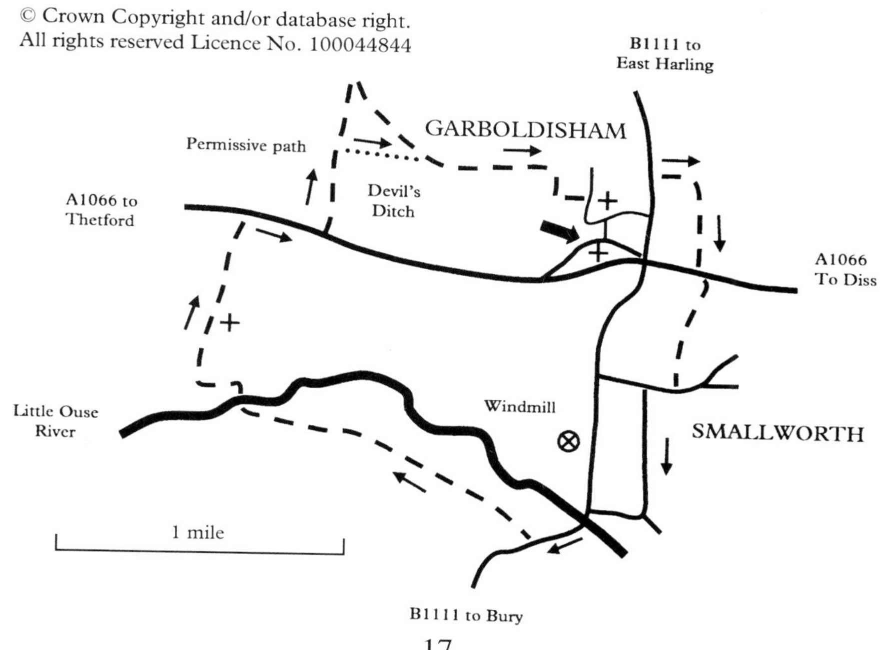

When you reach a house on the left, turn right onto a slightly sunken grass track leading gently uphill, leaving the route of the Angles Way behind. This path is a footpath though at the time of writing, (2005), was not signed. Follow the path over the hill, passing the tower of the ruined Saint Nicholas' Church on your right. This is virtually inaccessible as it is set in a thicket of scrub and trees. The path descends gently after the church, before climbing through an avenue of old oak and ash trees to pass between two houses to reach the A1066.

Unfortunately it is necessary to turn right and follow this busy road for about a quarter of a mile. However, the verge is wide enough to step onto along the length you walk to avoid traffic. Passing a wood on your right, and a tarmac lay-by, the road descends bearing right all the time. Now look for where a bridleway crosses the road and with the greatest care, turn left over the road onto a sunken track with the Devil's Ditch on the right.

Once safely away from the traffic this stretch is a pleasure to walk as it meanders uphill as a sunken track among trees with the Devil's Ditch beside you all the way. After a while the track emerges from the trees and runs alongside a field and a fence on your right. At a point where it jinks slightly right and left, turn right through a steel gate and onto a well maintained track which runs dead straight across the fields aiming for the corner of a block of woodland. ***NB This track is signed by the present landowner (2005) as a permissive path, the formal public footpath being awkward to use as the land is currently in use for stock rearing. The map shows the route of the official footpath as shown by the Ordnance Survey, as well as this permissive path.***

When you reach the corner of the wood go straight ahead keeping the wood on your right. After a while you reach woodland on the left as well, before the track runs out into farmland with a hedge on your right. Soon you come to another block of woodland on the right and at the far end of this turn right onto the signed bridle path with a small field to your left.

Pass the water abstraction borehole pump house on your right and then take the signed path left across the field towards the houses. This leads out into one of the village streets in Garboldisham and you turn right. Take the next left into Water Lane, dropping gently downhill passing the ruined tower that is all that remains of All Saints Church off to your left.

Look for the narrow footpath on your right which was the first path at the start of the walk and take this to return to your starting point by the church.

Did you know that....

William the Conqueror gave the area of **Garboldisham** to Hugh de Montford who had once been his standard bearer. At the time of the Domesday Book the name of 'Gerbodesham', as it was then spelt, applied to one of many manors that existed in the general area. These manors were united under a single lordship during the reign of Henry VIII. There are two churches in Garboldisham. That dedicated to **Saint John the Baptist** is still in use and certainly dates from the 11th century though its precise age is uncertain. The tower was started in 1463, records of this event being found in mediaeval wills. Inside the tower is a peal of six bells. A couple of hundred yards to the north stands a ruined tower which is all that remains of **All Saints Church**.

This church was in use until 1726 when, on the death of the then Rector, Thomas Vilet, services were discontinued. In 1734 approval was given to the abandoning of the upkeep of the church and the font and pews were removed along with the bells. The smallest bell was moved to Saint John's and the rest disposed of. The thatched and leaded roofs were removed and most of the fabric of the nave dismantled.

Quiet Lanes are an initiative of the Countryside Agency. Their objective is to make some rural roads more attractive for those who wish to walk, cycle or ride along them both for pleasure and for business. The concept is one of 'Share with Care' as it is recognised that traffic must still have access to them. In Norfolk the rural tranquillity of its country lanes is recognised and valued as a significant asset.

The **ruined church of St Nicholas** is in the parish of Gasthorpe. It was probably not in use after 1686 and according to White's *History, Gazetteer and Directory of Norfolk for 1845* the church had been in ruins for a long period even at that date. At the time Thomas Thornhill was Lord of the Manor and Patron of the church. Its present overgrown surroundings make access to the building impossible, though due to its ruinous condition perhaps this is just as well.

There are a number of ancient earthworks scattered throughout East Anglia with the name of **Devil's Ditch**. Many were built at the time of the invasions by the Danes in the 9th and 10th centuries as defences to protect main routes. This particular feature is only about two miles in length and runs from the marshy land in the valley of the nearby Little Ouse River northward to the higher ground towards East Harling.

4. Knettishall Heath Country Park and the Peddars Way

Grid reference of start TL956806 *Distance 7 miles*

Knettishall Heath Country Park is situated just south of the A1066 road about five miles east of Thetford. Turn right into the lane signed Coney Weston and follow the familiar brown tourist facility signs. There are three car parks available, all adjacent to the Rushford to Hopton road. For the purposes of this walk, park in the main car park by the crossroads just after you cross the **Little Ouse River bridge**. Check the closure time for the car parks which is displayed near their entrances. There is an information office which is open on most Sundays and Bank Holiday Mondays and there are also toilet facilities here. Picnic tables and way-marked trails are also in this area. The walk uses a section of the Peddars Way National Trail, which starts at Knettishall Heath, and also includes a section through the nearby Harling Woods. There are no refreshment opportunities along the route.

The Walk

Walk to the furthest end of the car park and continue ahead on the well defined path running parallel with the Hopton to Rushford lane on your left. This path crosses another less formal car park and continues straight ahead. After a while it divides but you can choose either route as they both eventually reach the signed Peddars Way route after passing through a small area of woodland.

Turn right onto the Peddars Way with a field on your left and descend to the Little Ouse which you cross by a wooden footbridge. Once over the river, follow the well defined path with conifers to the right and heathland to the left beyond a belt of scrubby trees. After a while the path follows the edge of the heath for a short distance and there are a number of interesting veteran oaks along this boundary. The path climbs gently with farmland on the right and a shelterbelt of pines, beech and oak on the left. When you reach the A1066 road, cross straight over to the road signed 'Peddars Way, Wretham 5 miles'. For a short distance you then walk on a redundant stretch of tarmac road through woodland to reach a country lane.

Here you turn right, moving away from the Peddars Way. When you reach the entrance road to the Forestry Commission's Thorpe Woodland Campsite on the left, take the unsigned track on the right which runs across the fields towards farm buildings straight ahead. When you reach the farm, turn left and follow the field edge for a short distance before jinking right onto a track along the edge of the forest. This is a public footpath signed by Norfolk County Council as a circular walk.

You soon leave the fields behind and have woodland on either side. This is the Forestry Commission's Harling Forest on West Harling Heath. When you reach the third turning on the left look carefully for the signed footpath striking off on the corner of the plantation. Initially this is a narrow path through the trees. After a short distance the path enters a small clearing in the plantation. The low mound in the centre of this clearing is a Bronze Age tumulus. This burial mound, which is a scheduled monument, is around 4000 years old and is some 36 metres in diameter and around two metres in height. The path soon joins a wider grassy track on which you continue ahead. At the next crossing of tracks go straight ahead with a beech plantation on your left. As you come to the end of the beech trees the path narrows again, crosses straight over a stony forest road and shortly passes through a belt of broadleaf trees to reach a lane. Turn right onto this lane and after about a hundred yards or so turn right, passing round a pole barrier, to re-enter the forest at a point opposite a wide sandy track on the left. Continue straight ahead on this track to reach a public road and turn right. ***(N.B. This track is the only section of the route which is not a public right of way. However, as it is on Forestry Commission freehold land with open access you have a permissive right to use it. In the rare event that it is closed due to forestry operations you can by-pass the track by remaining on the public roads as shown on the map).***

The lane is a long straight road but carries little traffic. When you reach the main A1066 road, cross straight over to walk down the tarmac drive leading to Riddlesworth Hall School. Ignore the entrance to the school on your right and continue straight ahead on the well signed footpath which passes the church on your left and then bears left becoming a gravelly drive once past the church. Very soon, look for the well signed footpath leading into the trees on your right at the end of a small strip of woodland.

You have now joined the Angles Way and this loops back through the trees to emerge on the headland of a field and is signed straight ahead. There is a good view of Riddlesworth Hall School along this section. Keep ahead along the headland of the field until you reach a grass track beside an attractive Cedar of Lebanon tree. Turn left on this track and follow it passing a small area of woodland on the right to reach a quiet lane. Turn left onto this and it will lead you back to the car park where you started the walk.

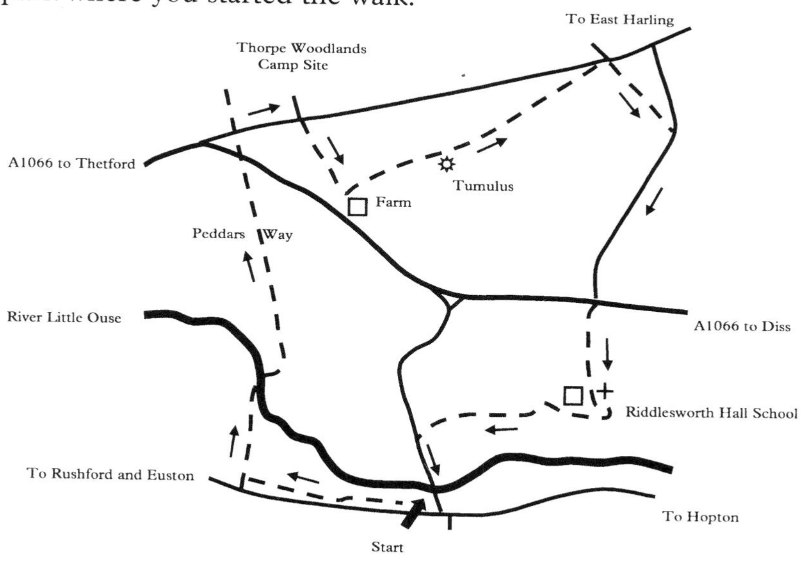

KNETTISHALL HEATH COUNTRY PARK

1 mile

Did you know that....

Knettishall Heath Country Park is owned and managed by Suffolk County Council. This large heath beside the River Little Ouse has two car parks and a number of circular, waymarked paths. It is also the starting point for the 95-mile long **Peddars Way** and Norfolk Coast Path National Trail. The **Icknield Way** Path and the **Angles Way**, (the latter a waymarked route between the Brecks and the Broads), also meet here. The Park is a mosaic of woodland, grass and heather heaths, some of which are grazed by sheep and Exmoor ponies at intervals in order to maintain the heath vegetation and prevent the encroachment of invasive scrub.

Riddlesworth Hall School is a private school offering nursery and preparatory education for boys and girls. Founded in 1946, the Georgian-style house stands in thirty acres of attractive parkland. Diana Spencer, later to become Princess of Wales, was once a pupil here.

The **Angles Way** is a regional long distance path which runs from Great Yarmouth to Knettishall Heath. The 77 mile long route runs via Breydon Water and Oulton Broad and then follows the route of the River Waveney to its source at Redgrave Fen. It then follows the Little Ouse, whose source is also close to Redgrave Fen, for the last few miles to Knettishall. It forms part of a connecting series of walks which form a 219 mile circuit of Norfolk. (Angles Way, Peddars Way, Norfolk Coast Path and the Weavers Way).

Hut Hill is a 4000 year old Bronze Age tumulus in the centre of the Park. A mound of this size may have as many as fifteen burials within it (graves or cremations), and they could all be membersd of a single important family of their time. The mound takes its name from a shepherd's hut which is thought to have been on or near the tumulus during the 19th century. Other features nearby include the remains of a circular rabbit warren. Until the 1950s, when myxomatosis decimated the rabbit population, the heath would have been virtually treeless. With virtually no rabbits to graze it, woodland plants such as pine, oak and birch have strongly invaded and today much of the heath is woodland. Although rabbit populations have slowly built up again, it is now necessary to use sheep and ponies to help maintain the most important areas of heath.

The Peddars Way National Trail is nearly 50 miles in length from its starting point on Knettishall Heath in Suffolk to Holme-next-the-Sea near Hunstanton. It is an ancient trackway, probably in existence before the Romans came, although in true Roman fashion they modified it and improved it considerably. In places the construction of the road, with its raised, cambered surface and shallow drainage gullies either side, (known as the Agger), can still be seen. It is now one of the long distance national trails which criss-cross much of England and connects with the **North Norfolk Coast Path**, another long distance path, near Hunstanton. The Way varies from narrow footpath to wide grassy track as you travel its length.

5. Barnham and the Icknield Way

Grid Reference of start TL 871792 *Distance 8 miles*

The start of this 8 mile walk is in Barnham village which is situated off the A134 road, three miles south of Thetford. The walk follows wide grassy paths and tracks over much of the route, though there are two very short sections along the wide verge of a main road. You can park on the straight stretch of road near the church in the main street in Barnham, taking care not to obstruct access to the church for services. The village sign depicts a windmill from the distant history of the village, a steam train from its more recent history and a jet fighter representing its connection with the nearby RAF camp and modern times. There are no refreshment opportunities on this walk so you will need to take your own food and drink.

The Walk

From the church walk back towards the Bury road taking the left fork beside the war memorial and which then passes the village hall on your left. At the main road turn right and walk towards Thetford for about a hundred yards until you are opposite a gap in the hedge with a Byway sign and not far from the traffic lights. This is a very fast and busy stretch of road, though fortunately you are only on it for a very short distance. Watch out for traffic and step back onto the verge while it passes.

Cross the road carefully and walk down the grassy Byway. The track is easy to follow though it jinks slightly left and right some way along with another Byway sign to confirm your route. After some little distance the track bears right and left as it passes through the demolished bridge of a disused railway.

Now follow the grassy track, through double gates, and keep straight ahead to join a tarmac lane which is also signed as a Byway. Here turn left and walk along the tarmac lane for several hundred yards passing cottages on your left. In time you will approach a fenced industrial area which is across the main track. Just before this a much smaller track slips off to the right and is signed as an official path diversion. Follow this path as it twists and climbs uphill, through trees, to bypass the industrial area. Near the top a splendid avenue of lime trees known as Duke's Ride crosses your path. Unfortunately this is not a right of way. Keep straight ahead over this to climb uphill and emerge into open fields.

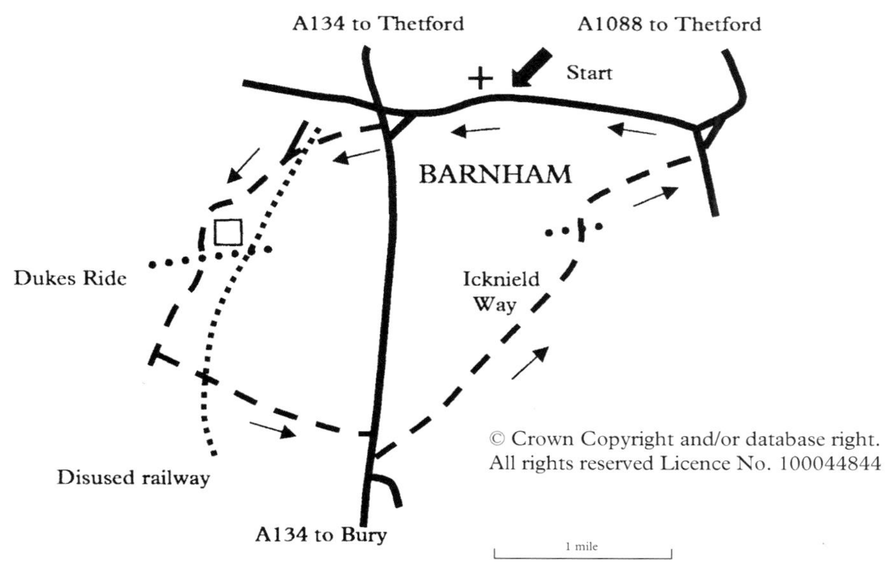

This stretch of track is open with excellent views over rolling countryside and is easy to follow. After some distance you will find another track off to the left signposted as the Icknield Way. This track crosses over the disused railway line before descending slightly and then climbing gently uphill, with a farm house on the right, to take you out eventually to reach the busy A134 Bury road. Again, turn right and walk about two hundred yards along the road, always being ready to climb onto the wide grass verge to avoid the traffic.

Just before the house on your left, the Icknield Way turns left down a tree-lined track and takes you back into the quiet of the countryside again. After some distance the track leaves the wooded section and once again you are on a wide grassy track with views across distant countryside. The path descends and then climbs again before beginning a long gentle descent. At the bottom of the slope at a crossing of paths, the main track bears away to the right as an entrance to a farm, but the Icknield Way is signed straight ahead taking you once more into a wooded section which continues gently downhill to reach a main road on the edge of the village of Euston.

On reaching the road, walk a few yards to the left to then turn left away from the main road and uphill on a much quieter lane. The last leg of the journey follows this lane for a little over a mile back to the place where you parked your car in Barnham.

Did you know that.....

The church of Saint Gregory in Barnham is worth a visit. Unusually, it is open during the day most of the time. The church was restored in the 19th century. The village of Barnham is worth walking around as it contains a number of older properties, many of which have thatched roofs. The large modern estate to the east of the main village was originally built to house families of servicemen based at nearby RAF Honington and Barnham Camp.

The Icknield Way is an ancient trackway running from Ivinghoe Beacon in Buckinghamshire to Knettishall Heath in Norfolk, a distance of about a 100 miles. It is thought to be the oldest road in England and certainly much of its length is pre-Roman. Archaeological features abound along its route as it follows the 'chalk spine' of England. In the south it links to the Ridgeway National Trail and Wessex while in Norfolk it connects to the Peddar's Way, another National Trail which crosses Norfolk to the coast near Hunstanton.

The **Bury to Thetford railway line** was constructed for the Thetford and Watton Railway Company in 1876. It was closed to passenger traffic in 1953 as part of the famous Beeching railway cuts and ceased freight haulage in 1960. After that the track was removed.

6. Troston and Great Livermere

Grid reference of start *TL897722* *Distance 6 miles*

The start of this walk is in the centre of Troston village. The village is reached from the A1088 Thetford to Ixworth road where it is signposted to the right shortly before you reach Ixworth. Food and drink are available from The Bull in Troston at the usual opening times.

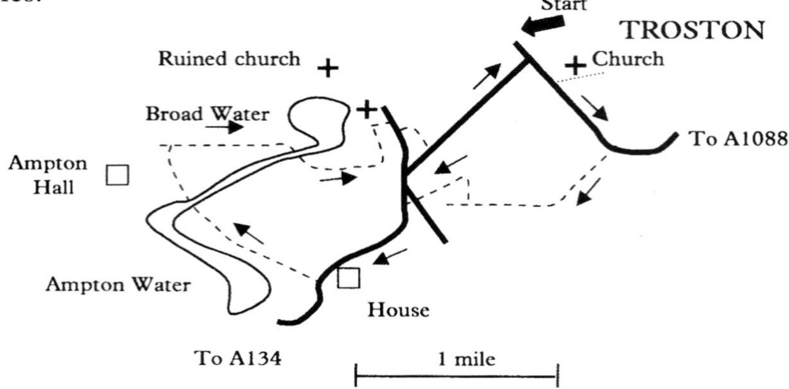

The Walk

Park in the main street opposite the entrance to the village hall. From here walk towards The Bull and take the turning left signposted Ixworth. Follow this lane for some distance passing Church Lane on your left. It is worth a short detour to visit the church of Saint Mary and to see the 15th century wall paintings which include the martyrdom of Saint Edmund and paintings of Saint Christopher and Saint George. Later along this lane you will pass Troston Hall on your left. Where the road bears hard left look for the Bridlepath sign on the right and follow this track out across fields keeping the hedge on your left.

At a T-junction cross a wooden bridge and turn right onto a wider grassy track signed as a R.U.P.P. (Road Used as a Public Path), and follow this gently downhill curving amongst individual poplar trees to right and left. Look out for another smaller wooden bridge on the right by a small footpath sign and follow the well-defined path between fields towards the corner of a wood. Just before the corner of the wood the path turns left to follow the edge of the wood on your right.

This is still a wide grassy track which brings you to a public road on the outskirts of Great Livermere village. Cross straight over and follow a short length of gravel track which quickly links to another public road. Turn left and follow this lane for some distance. Shortly after you pass a house on your left and pass between white railings on either side of the road, look for the footpath sign to the right.

From the sign you will see a wooden footbridge on the edge of a wood about a hundred yards or so across a field. You may find the footpath has been cultivated and planted with crops, in which case walk back a few yards and follow the edge of the field from the end of the white railings. Skirt the edge of the field and keep heading towards the wooden bridge and then take the signed footpath into the wood.

Once in the wood, keep straight ahead for some distance on a very well-defined path ignoring other paths to left and right. Soon you may hear the sound of wildfowl on your left and catch glimpses of a lake through the trees. Eventually the path moves away from the lake a little before climbing gently and then descending to the corner of a field on the right hand edge of the wood. There is a footpath sign at this point. A few more paces will bring you to the edge of Ampton Water and the view of a long narrow wooden bridge across it. You get a good view of Ampton Hall set in parkland across the water to the left as you cross this bridge.

Cross the lake and once on the other side go through the gap in the railings on your right and then turn left out into a field. Here you need to find a somewhat indistinct path which goes in a straight line up and over the hill moving gently away from the boundary of woodland and the railing fence. A power line crosses the horizon at the top of the hill and the path aims roughly at the centre of a span between poles.

Shortly after you pass under the line you reach a gravel road and a footpath sign on a short post.

Turn right and follow this track which is on high ground and gives good views over open countryside. You will see the tower of the ruined church of Little Livermere to the left beyond Broad Water, an extension of Ampton Water, and the church in Great Livermere ahead of you in the distance.

Keep to the gravel track, crossing over the lake, ignoring other signed footpaths to the left and head out to enter Great Livermere between a pair of estate gate-lodges.

Now turn left onto a short stretch of narrow tarmac road which quickly brings you to Saint Peter's church. This is well worth a visit.

You now need to seek out a footpath which goes right, away from the church and in front of a house at the end of the lane. This is not easy to see but there is a signpost indicating the path which is partly hidden in the trees. Follow this narrow hedged path a short distance to reach the main road in Great Livermere. Turn right and after about fifty yards along the pavement look for the next footpath signed on your left along a tarmac driveway between bungalows.

This bears right behind the bungalows and garages at their rear, becomes a gravel track and enters a grassy children's playground. Keep straight ahead along the hedge line by the side of the play area and look for the path exiting at the far corner to skirt a field at the rear of a house on your right.

On reaching the main road, turn left and follow the lane for about ten minutes walk back to Troston.

Did you know that....

The thatched **church of Saint Peter in Great Livermere** dates mainly from the 13th century though almost certainly earlier churches have occupied the site since the 7th century. The tower, which probably took more than ten years to construct, is thought to have been finished at the end of the 12th century. The upper stage of the original tower collapsed during a storm in 1871. A peal of five bells, which when they were cast in 1762 was the lightest peal of five in the world, is still rung on special occasions. Paintings on the plaster of interior walls date from the 13th and 14th centuries. The screen, which was once probably richly decorated, dates from the 15th century. The interior is plain and without any stained glass, reflecting its development in a simple and small community but it is beautifully kept by its present parishioners.

Ampton Water is a large artificial lake in the parkland of Ampton Hall. It is connected to Broad Water by the long narrow stretch known as Long Water. The footpath across the Long Water is a long narrow bridge with a raised section in the middle to allow punts and other small boats to move up and down the length of the lake. There is a fine view of Ampton Hall as you cross the bridge.

The ruined **church of Saint Peter and Saint Paul, Little Livermere**, has been ruinous since the early 20th century. Its tower was raised to its exceptional height in the past to make it visible across the estate. It stands on private ground and there is no public access.

7. Culford and West Stow

Grid reference of start TL839705 *Distance 4 miles*

The start of this walk is from the village of Culford which is situated on the B1106 between Bury St Edmunds and Elveden. An important feature of the village is Culford School which lies along one side of the main street through the village. There are no refreshment facilities on this comparatively short walk.

Park in the car park at the rear of the village hall, which is behind the War Memorial. Please park thoughtfully as this parking area may be required for village events. If the car park is unavailable for this reason, park carefully along the main street through the village. Please note that walkers use this car park at their own risk.

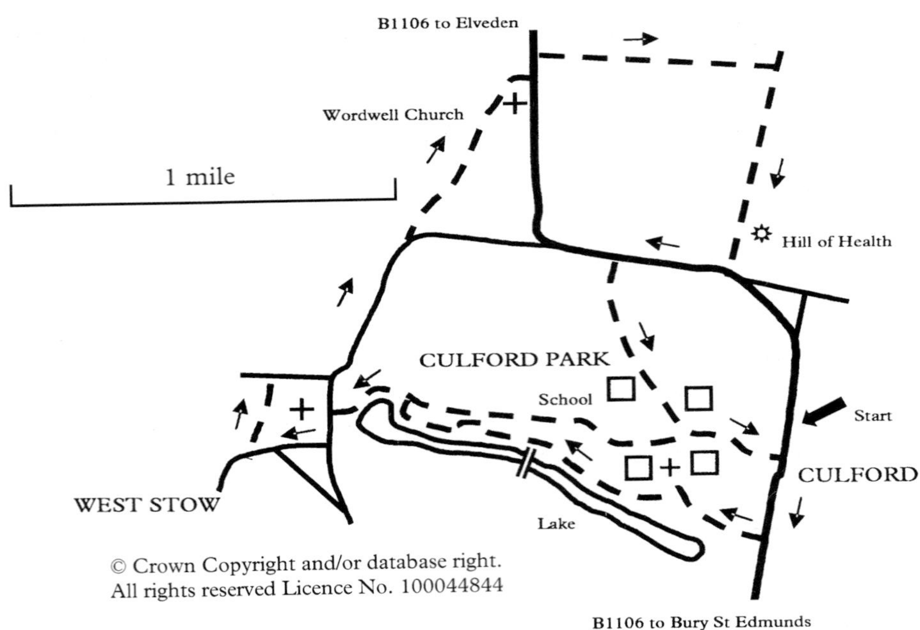

The Walk

There are two entrances to Culford School, both of which are public footpaths as well as providing vehicular access to the school. It is possible to start the walk from either entrance, (see map). However, for the purposes of describing the walk I suggest you use the entrance at the Bury St Edmunds end of the village, which follows the marked route of the Lark Valley Path for some distance.

Walk down the main street to enter the grounds of Culford School through the wrought iron entrance gates at the Bury St Edmunds end of the village. Continue along a tarmac drive through lawns and parkland, and after you pass a modern bungalow on the right and just before reaching the church, look for the signed gravel footpath off to the left heading towards trees.

With the church on your right follow the path as it bears off to the left signed as the Lark Valley Path. This section of the path is also signed as David Anderson's Way. Keep straight ahead on a well-mown path between trees and where it forks take the left hand fork which brings you out into a clearing on the banks of a lake. Turn right here and follow the path along the side of the lake. There are good views of Culford Hall as you walk along this stretch of the walk. Pass the cricket field and pavilion on your right and a small stone and iron bridge over the lake on your left.

Keep straight ahead, crossing a stile and picking up signs for the Lark Valley Path. The path is still a good walking route though now it passes through scrubbier areas with trees and in the distance you can see the tower of West Stow church partly hidden by trees. The path comes up against a fenced area which is a Biology Field Study area for Culford School. Simply turn right and follow the fence line around this area and you soon return to the lakeside.

Keep ahead with the lake to your left. The path on this section is less distinct but as long as you follow the lake you will be on the route. The path follows the curve of the lake and after crossing a stile it meets with a gravelled driveway onto which you turn left. (N.B. this driveway accommodates the other possible route for the start of the walk described earlier). The driveway crosses the head of the lake over its outlet sluice with a stream on your right which will eventually flow into the River Lark some distance beyond the route of this walk.

Just after the sluice the Lark Valley Path is signed off to the right and runs for a short distance along the rear of houses to emerge on a public road. Immediately opposite is the entrance to West Stow church.

Turn left along the lane, still following the Lark Valley Path signs and take the first turning right onto another quiet road at a point opposite a pair of flint cottages which were once gatehouses on either side of the carriage drive to Culford Hall. Another road joins from the left signed By Road and at the point where your road bears quite sharply left look for the signed footpath on the right though a gap in the hedge. (This is where the route leaves the Lark Valley Path behind and continues its circuit on standard rights of way).

Almost immediately, climb a stile into parkland. Keep straight across aiming for the footpath sign on a post about seventy yards ahead and a further sign over by the corner of the field where there is a post and rail fence. The footpath is signed left here into the trees. Go though a gate and cross a bridge over a very small stream and bear right to follow the path keeping a field with railings to your left. The path widens and has a railing fence on each side and climbs uphill, crossing a stile, to meet the road in the village of West Stow.

Turn right and follow the lane until it reaches a T-junction at which point you turn left. Follow this lane for about half a mile and at a point where it bears hard right look for the footpath sign on your left. Cross yet another stile and turn right to follow the field edge with a hedge and garden on your right.

At the end of the field there is a junction with other fields. Go through the gap in the fence on your right and then bear left, slightly diagonally across the field, aiming for another stile just visible in front of trees. Go over the stile and a small bridge over a drainage ditch and walk uphill a short distance to another stile.

Cross this stile and walk straight across the next field, aiming at the left hand corner of Wordwell church, visible at the top of the hill. On reaching the church, follow the boundary round keeping the churchyard on your right before crossing a stile to reach a main road.

Turn left on this road and walk a short distance along, keeping to the verge until you reach the driveway to Wordwell Hall. Here you turn right and cross the road to follow the signed footpath as it climbs steadily uphill. This is the highest point on the walk with good views back over the countryside you have just walked through.

Near the brow of the hill you go through a gap in the hedge and into a second field and head towards the right hand corner of a small wood. The footpath goes into the wood keeping close to the edge for about twenty yards and then emerges as a track along the edge of a field with the wood on the left. You eventually leave this wood behind but soon pick up another which you skirt in the same way to reach a gravel track.

Turn right and walk downhill on this track which becomes a concrete drive for the last twenty yards or so to reach main road. As you come down the hill on this track look for the large round mound with old pine trees on it on the left in a garden. This is a Bronze Age tumulus or burial mound known as The Hill of Health.

At the main road turn right. You now have to walk for about a quarter of a mile along this road which can be fairly busy at times. However it is straight, with good visibility, and you can easily climb on to the grassy verge along the entire length you are walking if traffic approaches.

Look out for a signed footpath on the left and follow this uphill with a fence on your left and heading towards a tall brick-built water tower partly hidden by trees. Just before you reach the tower there is a small building which once held a pump to raise underground water to fill the tower. Carry on past both buildings and the footpath enters a small wood.

You emerge from the wood onto some sports fields belonging to Culford School, with the footpath signed with a yellow arrow on a small post pointing diagonally across a rugby field to a similar post between two large beech trees. This in turns leads to another post on the left of an ancient stag-headed oak enclosed by iron railings. Finally, complete the crossing of the sports fields and parkland, with views of Culford Hall to your right, by aiming towards a three-fingered footpath signpost alongside the tarmac drive through Culford School.

Once on the drive way, you turn left and follow the signs to the exit and you will then return to the main street in Culford village where you started the walk.

Did you know that....

Culford School came into being in1935 when the then East Anglian School for Boys moved out of Bury St Edmunds where it had been since 1881. The school subsequently merged with the East Anglian School for Girls in 1972. Today it is an independent co-educational school for day and boarding pupils aged between 2 and 18. Culford Hall, which is part of the school complex, was once the home of the Benyon and later the Cadogan families. It stands in a 480 acre estate landscaped by Humphrey Repton in the 18th century.

The Lark Valley Path is a waymarked path linking Bury St Edmunds to Mildenhall following the tiny River Lark, along whose banks it passes for much of the route. The River Lark navigation was created by Act of Parliament in 1700 and allowed for the Lark to be made navigable by boat between Mildenhall and Fornham, near Bury St Edmunds.

The **church of Saint Mary, Culford** stands in the landscaped parkland of Culford School. It was built in 1850 on the site of an earlier church with money provided by the then Lord of the Manor, Edward Richard Benyon of Culford Hall.

The **church of St Mary, West Stow**, was built largely in the 14th and 15th centuries, but was derelict by the 19th century and was much restored to its present condition in Victorian times.

The **church of All Saints, Wordwell** is largely Norman in origin. By the beginning of the 19th century it had fallen into disuse but was restored in the 1850s. Today it is in the care of the Churches Conservation Trust. The church is normally locked but details of local key-holders are given on the church notice board.

8. Mildenhall and Tuddenham

Grid reference of start TL 714745 *Distance 8 miles*

This walk starts from the main car park off Jubilee Way which is at the end of King's Street in the centre of Mildenhall. King's Street is behind the war memorial. Mildenhall is an attractive small market town with a number of shops and places to eat and drink. The church with its tall tower dominates the town centre and the **historic market cross** is one of the historical features to be seen. There are further refreshment opportunities in Tuddenham and Barton Mills part way around the walk.

The Walk

From the car park continue down Jubilee Way, passing the Jubilee Centre on your left and picking up the signed Lark Valley Path leading down to the River Lark. On reaching the river, turn left and follow the river bank on a good, surfaced path. This path leads you to the A11 dual carriageway. Cross straight over with the greatest care and continue along the riverside path which is a grassy path on this side of the road.

When the path reaches the Cut-Off Channel, cross this by following the pathway over the sluice and resume the route along the main river bank. Keep to this path for some distance and, shortly after you pass a weir, turn right to cross the river over a bridge. Keep straight ahead, climbing gently uphill on a fenced gravel track across Cavenham Heath. After a while this becomes a quiet tarmac road that leads you into the village of Tuddenham.

Turn right by the green on to the main road through the village. This bears left past the White Hart pub and leaves the village passing Tuddenham Mill on the left. After this, take the second public road on the left. There is no direction sign for this lane but it climbs steadily uphill for some distance, much of it through woodland on either side. On the top of the hill take the track on the right opposite another country lane. This track leads out onto higher ground with excellent views across to the churches at Barton Mills and Mildenhall and with the buildings at RAF Mildenhall beyond. Through the shelter belts to the right you can see the valley of the River Lark which you walked along earlier on the walk.

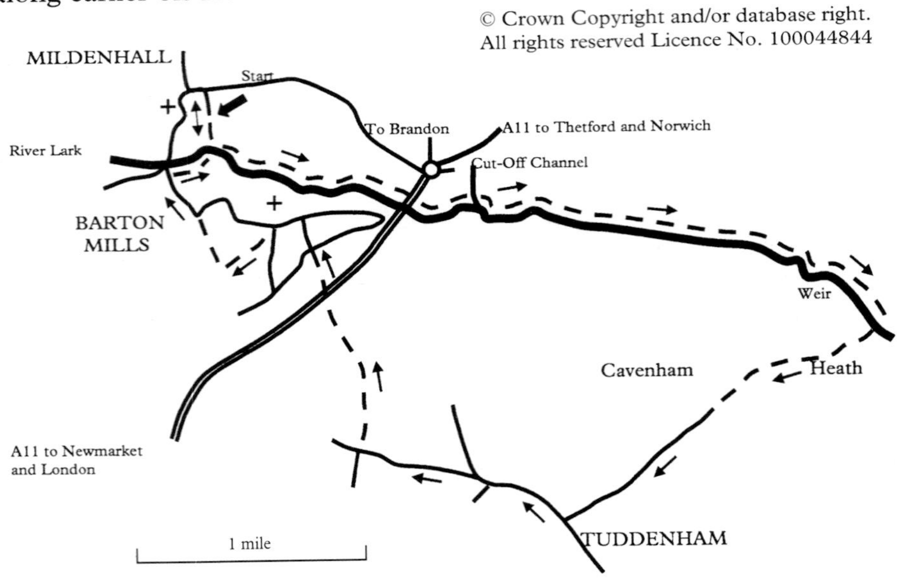

The track bears left and drops downhill to meet the A11 again. Cross with care (on this occasion there is a gap in the crash barrier to make it easier) as this is a fast and usually busy road. Once across pick up the track which aligns with the one you have just left and continue towards a quiet public road in Barton Mills.

Cross straight over this road into Bell Lane and then turn left into The Street. As you pass the parish church, fork left into Grange Lane which is on the corner of Church Lane. This takes you past the recreation ground on your right. As you leave the houses behind, pass through a field gate onto a stony track with fields on either side. This track meets another and you turn right onto a short stretch of earth track with farm buildings on your left before joining a tarmac drive and going through another field gate.

Follow this driveway until it meets a public road on a bend. Continue straight ahead along this lane. Just before you reach the main road, look for the signed public footpath on your right. This path is also the driveway to houses and follows the river on the left. At the end of the drive pick up the path along the river and then, after crossing two footbridges, turn left to retrace your steps up the track to the car park at the start of the walk.

Did you know that.....

The origins of **Mildenhall** date back to Anglo Saxon times and at the Domesday survey there were 64 families living there. A Royal Charter was granted in 1412 for a weekly market to take place. The Mildenhall Treasure is one of the most famous finds in the country. It comprises some 34 silver articles unearthed near West Row in 1943 by a local ploughman, Gordon Butcher. The hoard, which dates back to 4th century Roman Britain, was pronounced Treasure Trove in 1946 and is now housed in the British Museum. You can get more information about the history of the local area from the **Mildenhall Museum** in King Street. Admission is free. There is a significant American population in the area due to the proximity of nearby RAF Mildenhall and Lakenheath air bases. There was an air strip at Mildenhall between the wars and George V took the Silver Jubilee Review there in 1935.

Cavenham Heath National Nature Reserve, which is 204 hectares in extent, is managed by English Nature. It is one of the most diverse of the remaining Breck heaths, being mainly dry acidic heath but with some damper areas near to the River Lark, as well as grass heath where the soils are chalkier. Nearby Roper's Field was successfully reverted from arable land to grass heath in recent years.

The Cut-Off Channel runs from the River Lark at Barton Mills to the River Great Ouse at Denver Sluice in the Fens. It was completed in 1964 as part of the flood protection system to protect the Fens following the serious floods of 1947. It acts as a catchment for the rivers which drain from the higher ground to the east of the Fens. A system of sluices and pumps allows water movement to be controlled to guard against the risk of flooding of the low-lying areas of the Fens. In addition water can also be transferred south to the Rivers Stour, Blackwater and Colne as well as into reservoirs in Essex.

Each summer for a number of years Barton Mills has hosted a **Scarecrow Festival** and villagers join in to provide dozens of different, and often highly amusing, scarecrows which decorate their gardens, houses and other buildings. This event, usually held over a weekend in June, has become hugely popular and large numbers of visitors come to see the spectacle and at the same time raise funds for local charities.

9. Weeting and Brandon

Grid reference of start *TL 775885* *Distance 4 miles*

The start of this walk is in the centre of the village of Weeting. From Brandon town take the A1065 towards Mundford and immediately after the level crossing fork left onto the Weeting road. Keep to the main road through the village and immediately after you pass the village sign on its flint plinth, turn left into a parking area beside the bowls club.

The Saxon pub and the local shop are not far from the start of the walk and offer opportunities for refreshments. It is also easily possible to make a short diversion into Brandon for the same purpose part of the way around the walk.

The Walk

Start by walking left behind the bowls club building and along a road with houses on the left. This leads to the Hockwold road; continue straight onto this for a short distance. When this road bends sharp right carry on straight ahead down a stony track passing Shadwell Close on your left.

This track jinks right and left between houses, passing Fengate Farm and a long brick wall on the right before heading off into open country. Soon it bears fairly sharply left, becoming a sandy track with buildings visible in the distance.

As you reach the buildings, the track becomes a tarmac road running through a small industrial area to reach a main road. At this point if you turn right a short walk will take you into Brandon town centre with its shops and refreshment opportunities. However, the walk itself turns left to follow the long straight road towards Weeting, passing Brandon Catholic Church on the left. Fortunately there is a pavement alongside this stretch of road.

When you reach the thirty miles per hour restriction signs turn right at the cross roads, signposted Mundford, onto a quieter lane. Follow this for about a hundred and fifty yards, looking for a gate on the left beside a footpath sign. (A short distance further along the lane is Pepper's Hill, a Bronze Age tumulus clearly visible at the edge of the lane.)

Go through the gate and walk straight away from the road on a sandy track with some woodland nearby. For a while there is a small scrubby wood on your right followed by open fields heading towards another wood on the left. Continue straight ahead keeping tight to the edge of the wood along the sandy track. At a point where a wider shelterbelt of trees is on your right the track divides and you keep straight ahead, which essentially is the right fork at this junction.

The sandy track continues to the corner of a large block of woodland, which is part of Thetford Forest. Another track joins from the right and you turn left to the corner of the wood with a farm cottage visible in front of you. Turn right and, after a short distance, left, thus avoiding the track which is the entrance road to the house. You will find 'Weeting Village Walks' signs on small discs fastened to trees or short posts in this area and they guide you past the house. The track becomes a stony road and immediately past another farm and buildings on the left, it divides. You need to turn left onto a bridle path which is the Pilgrim's Walk and straight ahead is yet another rather larger collection of farm buildings.

When you arrive at these buildings the right of way bears right to circle and avoid most of the buildings, including a farm house, to arrive at Weeting Parish Church and the entrance to the ruins of Weeting Castle on the left.

Carry on straight ahead as the track becomes a tarmac road passing a residential area to reach the village green at Weeting. Here there is a small shelter and an extremely detailed and useful board with lots of information about the village and its surroundings.

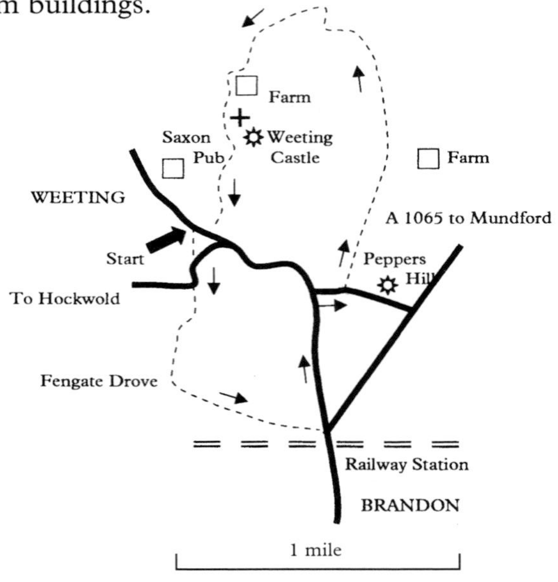

Cross the green heading towards the long row of thatched cottages and you will see the flint plinth and village sign off to your right with the parking area where you started the walk. There are two unusually large walnut trees on the verge close to the village sign.

Did you know that....

Weeting Castle was built in 1130 by William de Warrenne, son-in-law to William the Conqueror, on the site of an earlier 10th century settlement. It is a fortified, moated manor house rather than a castle and was abandoned in the 14th century. Today it is managed by English Heritage.

The church of Saint Mary is the village's surviving church. Soon after 1700 the tower of the other church of All Saints collapsed on the nave and destroyed it. Some remains of this lost church are still visible in the form of bumps and mounds in the grass in a corner of the recreation ground.

Weeting is famous for its **steam and traction engine rally**, which takes place in July each year and has been a feature of village life for more than thirty years. More than 100 steam traction engines gather at the venue, making it one of the largest of its kind to be held in the country. Many of the old steam engines were constructed at the famous Burrell factory in Thetford and you can visit the museum housed in the old paint shop in the town.

Pepper's Hill is a tumulus or burial mound dating from the Bronze Age and is around three thousand years old. It is situated alongside a stretch of the **Harling Drove**, a track of some antiquity, which links Hockwold on the edge of the fens in the west with East Harling across the heaths and forest in the east.

The terrace of thatched cottages opposite the school is known as **The Row.** The cottages date from 1770 and are reputed to have the longest single span thatched roof in England.

A mile or so out of the village on the Hockwold road is the **Weeting Heath National Nature Reserve**. This is an important fragment of Breckland Heath valued for its population of breeding stone curlews and rare Breckland plants. It is accessible, by permit, at certain times of the year and there is a small visitor centre adjacent to the road.

10. Oxborough and Gooderstone

Grid reference of start TF744045 *Distance 6 miles*

The walk starts in the village of Oxborough which is most easily reached via the A134 Thetford to King's Lynn road where it is clearly signed from the Stoke Ferry by-pass. The village is on the boundary between Breckland and the fens and some of the walk is on low-lying ground, though the majority of the route is clearly Breckland in character. You can park in one of the quiet roads close to the village green. Bar meals and other refreshments can be obtained from the Bedingfield Arms in Oxborough and The Swan in Gooderstone, part way around the route.

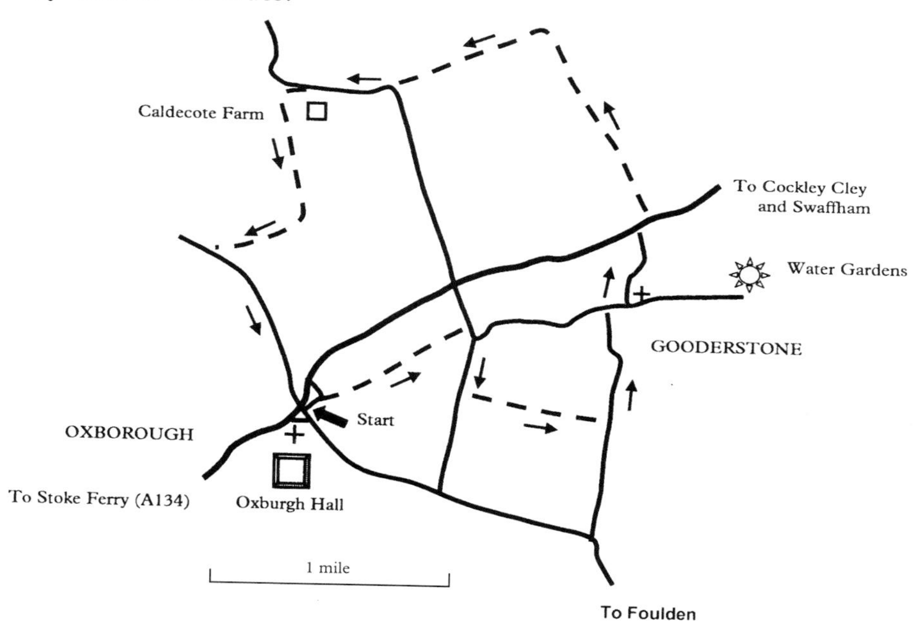

The Walk

Take the road along the edge of the green, keeping the Bedingfield Arms on your right and continue away from the green down the narrow road straight ahead passing the village post office on your left. This is a No Through Road, so after a short distance turn right down the signed footpath between houses with a fence on your left. Cross the stile and turn left along the field headland. Leaving the houses behind, keep straight ahead on the signed footpath with a hedge on your right. After a couple of hundred yards the path dog-legs and you cross a stile into a field with the hedge now on your left. Aim diagonally across this rather narrow, rough pasture towards the buildings associated with a small sewage treatment works visible at the far end of the field. With the buildings on your right, cross a stile and turn right into a quiet lane, almost immediately crossing a bridge over the tiny River Gadder.

After crossing the river turn right into Chalk Row Lane and follow this straight road for about a quarter of a mile; then, opposite some farm buildings on your right, take the signed bridleway on the left. The bridleway is a grassy track initially with a hedge on the right, but as it climbs gently uphill it becomes hedged on both sides. On reaching the lane at the end of the track, turn left and follow the lane into the village of Gooderstone. This is a quiet lane with a wide verge on either side.

On reaching the main street in the village, turn right and then, just before reaching the church, turn left into Clarke's Lane. The Swan public house is opposite the church. You soon cross over the little River Gadder again and on reaching a T-junction turn right, signed Cockley Cley. After about a hundred yards take the signed bridleway on the left which is a grassy track between fields with a hedge on the left.

The grassy track goes over the brow of a hill and becomes a stony track with a house off to your right. Immediately after passing the house, the track is hedged by Breck pines on the right. The track bears left sharply and you follow this track, now hedged on both sides, until you reach a lane.

You reach this lane on a bend, with the road to Gooderstone and Oxborough signed off to the left. However, keep straight ahead and pass Caldecote Farm on the left. As you approach the end of the farm buildings the lane bears away to the right and you continue straight ahead on a sandy track. After a hundred yards or so this track bears hard left and continues ahead with a hedge on your left before becoming a tree-lined track, which can be rather muddy in winter, a little further on. Just before the track meets with a wood in front of you, turn right onto a wide grassy track across open fields. The wood is signed as in use for paintball war games.

When this track reaches another quiet lane, turn left and follow it for a little over half a mile back to Oxborough and the start of your journey.

Did you know that....

Oxburgh Hall was built in 1482 by the Bedingfield family and their descendants are still in residence here today. This moated Tudor house with its magnificent gatehouse and mysterious priest hole is today managed by the National Trust and is open to visitors during the summer season and for special events during the rest of the year. The gardens include a parterre, walled orchard and woodland walks.

The church of Saint John the Evangelist, Oxborough, is located in the centre of the village close to the boundary wall of the hall. At first site it may appear to be partly ruinous. This is because the tower of the original church collapsed in April 1948 destroying the roof of the nave as it fell. The tower had a spire rising to over a hundred and fifty feet in height which was struck by lightning in 1877 and rebuilt in stone in 1879. It was thought that the combined weight of this stone tower with its six bells contributed to its collapse. Today the chancel alone serves as a church but one of significant proportions. The Bedingfield Chapel was built onto the side of the chancel around

1500. The Chapel is famous for the terracotta stonework screens it contains. They are rare in England and of fine quality, being made of screened brick clay, moulded and then fired. They date from 1525 to 1550 and were probably made by French craftsmen trained by Italian masters.

William the Conqueror acquired *Gudestuna*, as it was then known, and granted it to Godric his steward. **The church of Saint George, Gooderstone** was built around 1200 and contains much unspoilt medieval architecture and other fittings. The south porch is 14th century and the tower dates from the 13th and 14th centuries. It contains 3 bells which date from 1625 and 1710.

Gooderstone Water Gardens were created from a wet meadow in 1970 by Billy Knights, a retired local farmer, and his wife Florence. They are six acres in extent and situated alongside the crystal clear waters of the tiny River Gadder, a trout stream. Today they contain four ponds, thirteen bridges and a considerable length of waterway all accessed by a network of grass paths set among mature trees. There are also tea rooms, toilets and various seating facilities and the gardens are open daily until 5.30 pm (dusk in winter).

11. Beachamwell and its Churches

Grid reference of start TF 751053 *Distance 5 or 7 miles*

Beachamwell is signed from the A1122 (A47) Swaffham to Downham Market road. You can park easily in the centre of the village near the large village green. Refreshments can be obtained from the village pub, The Great Danes, which is open at the usual times. The walk has good views of the surrounding countryside as well as taking in the sites of two of Beachamwell's ruined churches.

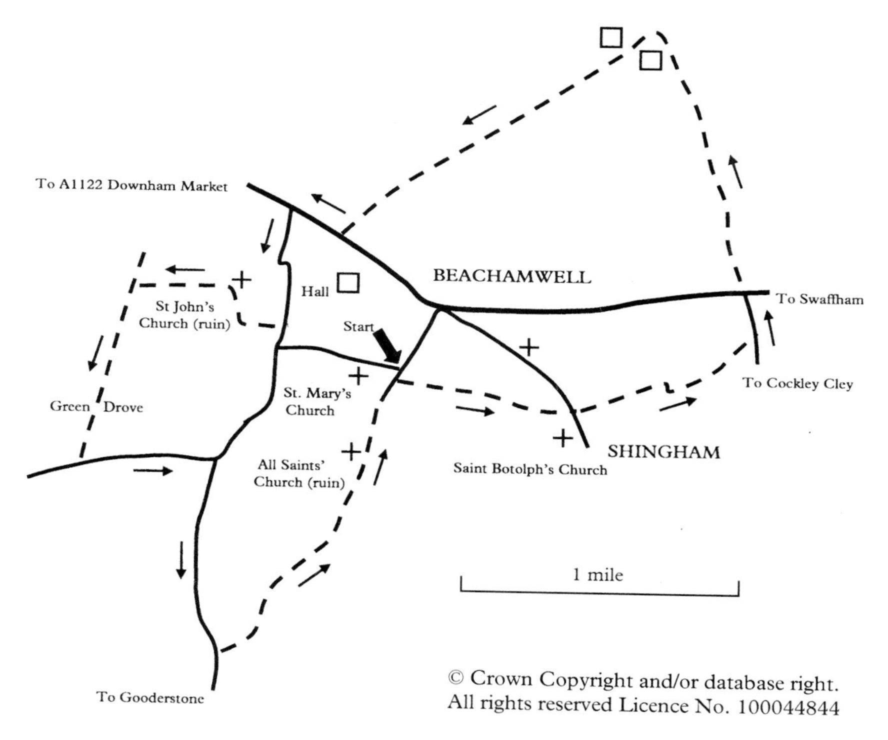

The Walk

To start the walk take the narrow path immediately beside The Great Danes pub. Although not signed off of the village street, it is easy to find and runs between a house and a tall wooden fence for a short distance.

As you leave the houses behind, the path is signed to run alongside a field with a hedge on the right. It then runs through a wood, keeping just inside the edge of the wood. Ignore the other signed footpath which goes off to the left in the wood.

You leave the trees by crossing a small wooden footbridge and go through a gate to emerge into a field. The path is signed and clearly well used and crosses the field going through another gate to reach a lane. This is the tiny hamlet of Shingham and a few yards down the lane to the right is the entrance to the redundant church of Saint Botolph, which is of Norman origin. Originally the nave had a thatched roof but today it is covered in copper sheet for protection. Go straight across the lane down a track with a footpath sign and houses on the left.

At the end of the houses the path jinks left and right and becomes a grass path between fields with a hedge on your right. At the end of the hedge the path then dog-legs right and left, and continues straight ahead with another hedge on the left and an area of woodland straight ahead. Ignore the signed footpath which goes off to the right across the field.

The path passes through the wood as a grassy track which leads out to a country lane. Incidentally this wood is an Arboretum, a collection of trees and shrubs, which was planted by a local farmer and haulier some years ago. It is now a fascinating area with trees of many species to be seen as you pass through. When you reach the lane turn left.

Soon you come to a T-junction of public roads and here go straight across onto a signed bridleway which is a stony track at this point. Where the track divides take the right fork passing a house and gardens on the left. Ignore the next turning on the right and keep straight ahead. At the end of the wood keep straight ahead on a sandy track which is the headland to the field on your left.

Keep to the sandy track which jinks right and left at the brow of the hill and then picks up the boundary of Swaffham Forest on your right. The track continues straight ahead with buildings visible in the distance among trees on the brow of the next hill. When you reach the cross track near the buildings turn left with the ruins of a building among the trees on the left and a cottage on the right. The sandy track then sets straight off across fields.

After some distance the track becomes a stony one with a wood on the right and a shelterbelt on the left. Continue straight ahead, climbing gently uphill, ignoring the signed footpath to right and left which crosses your route. You pass another wood on the right and then the track, which by now is a well-made stony farm road, continues ahead with a hedge on your left.

The track reaches a lane almost opposite the entrance drive to Beachamwell Hall. Turn right and, after a short distance, left into a lane signed to Beachamwell. This lane twists and turns past the buildings of Saint John's Farm on your right and then straightens out. Across the fields to the right you get a good view of the **ruins of Saint John's Church**. Some way down the straight stretch look for the signed footpath going off across the field on the right. It passes between two large Corsican pine trees which are a good landmark.

(N.B. At this point you could take a short cut back to Beachamwell by continuing straight ahead down this lane and turning left into The Street if you wanted to shorten your walk).

Walk across this narrow field and climb the stile into another field. The path is signed diagonally off to the right but is far from obvious on the ground! The best bet is to aim to walk through the centre of a clump of mature trees in the middle of the field and once there you will see the next stile and footpath sign straight ahead. From here there is a closer view of the ruined church.

Cross the stile and continue straight ahead with the church behind you and a good track along the headland of the fields and a hedge on the right. When you cross a third stile turn left onto a hedged grassy track known as the Green Drove. Ignore the footpath which is signed to cross straight over The Drove as you cross the stile.

At the end of The Drove, cross the earth bank which prevents vehicles from using it and turn left into a quiet lane. Follow this lane and turn hard right at a junction signed Gooderstone and Oxborough.

Follow the lane passing a wood and a pumping station on your right. The lane bears left and drops gently downhill. Just before it then bears right, look for the gap in the hedge on the left with the signed public path indicated. This is a wide grassy path which is very distinct as it crosses the fields for some distance. Ignore the signed footpath off to the left and keep ahead to pass through a gate.

The track is well used and very obvious as it bears left to pass the ruins of All Saints Church. It then follows the boundary of the garden of a large converted barn on the left, joins the gravelled drive which is the entrance to the barn and continues straight ahead towards Beachamwell village. As you reach the houses the lane becomes a tarmac road called Old Hall Lane which leads you back to the start of the walk.

Did you know that....

According to the Domesday Book, **Beachamwell** was once two villages, '*Wella* and *Bitcham*'. Wella's remains have been identified near the ruins of All Saints' Church on the southern outskirts of the present village. This is an ancient community with prehistoric tools and Roman and Saxon artefacts found in the locality as well as the Devil's Dyke earthwork nearby. As well as All Saints and the present church of Saint Mary there were three others; Saint John's, whose remains are clearly visible in farmland along the walk, Saint Botolph's, situated in the nearby hamlet of Shingham and a Wesleyan chapel, also in Shingham and now converted into a house.

Today Beachamwell's only church is that of **Saint Mary**. The church has a thatched roof and a Saxon round tower with a later hexagonal upper section. An interesting carving on one of the pillars in the nave is that of the Beachamwell Demon, seen sticking his tongue out at the members of the congregation! The church overlooks the large village green and faces the village pub at the other end of the green.

The Great Danes Country Inn, formerly the Cooper's Arms, has been a public house since at least 1821. It closed in 1974 and was reopened around 1977. At some time it was also known as The Hole in the Wall because drinkers obtained their ale without entering the building via a hole in the side wall and drank outside.

You may well see and hear Tornado jets from nearby **RAF Marham** during the walk. The construction of Marham airfield began in 1935 and 38 Squadron was the first to be based there operating Fairy Hendon bombers. In 1982, 617 Squadron began operating Tornado GR1 aircraft at Marham. Today, the station is home to four squadrons of Tornado GR4s and a Canberra reconnaissance squadron. The Tornado Multi Role Combat Aircraft, (MRCA), is currently the RAF's principal strike aircraft and can fly at more than twice the speed of sound (Mach 2.2).

12. Ashill and South Pickenham

Grid reference of start   TF 887046   *Distance 5 miles*

This walk starts in Ashill village which lies on the B1077 between Watton and Swaffham. Take the Holme Hale road and you will find plenty of parking space around the green in the centre of the village. Refreshments are available at the White Hart pub in the village at the usual opening times.

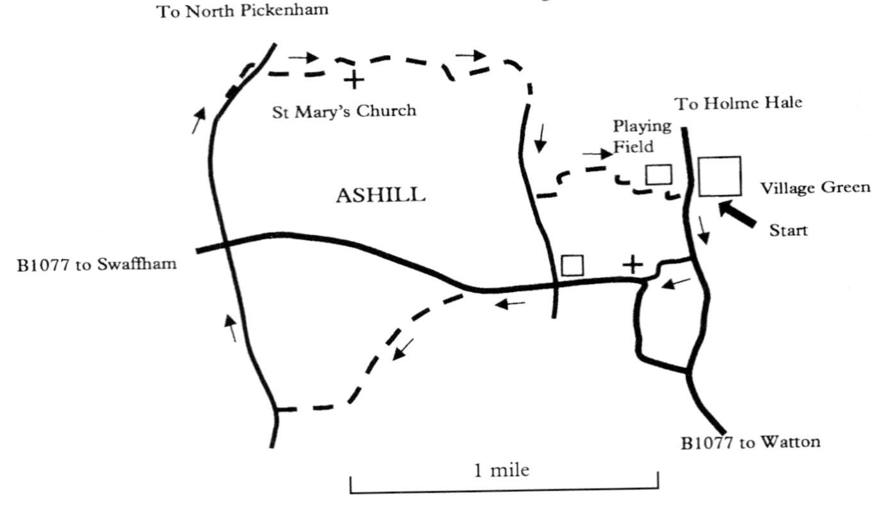

The Walk

From the green turn left onto the main road through the village. At this point the road is called Hale Road but soon becomes Watton Road as you pass through the village. Turn right opposite the school into Church Road, which passes the White Hart pub and a number of interesting old cottages to reach the church of Saint Nicholas.

Here you keep straight ahead along the pavement beside the main road. When you reach the cross roads by a small group of houses, continue straight ahead. For the next couple of hundred yards or so follow the lane, looking out for the finger post indicating a bridle path just past a building on your left. Take this track which soon becomes a grass path along the field headland with a hedge on your left. This drops gently downhill, picking up another field where the slope starts to level out and continues ahead to reach a lane. Turn right onto the lane. This is a very quiet road which is also the designated route for the Peddars Way at this point. It climbs gently uphill with views across parkland and mature trees to Pickenham Hall on your left.

At the cross roads with a more major road, go straight ahead still gently uphill. You will pass a concrete farm loading area on your left and about two hundred yards after that the Peddars Way is signposted off the lane to the left to run as a footpath along the field edge with the hedge on your right. At the end of the first field go through the gap in the hedge, cross the road and take the track opposite, signed to Saint Mary's Church.

This stony track climbs steadily uphill, keeping to the field edge and with fine views across the surrounding countryside as you near the top. This is one of the highest points in this part of the Breckland. You can see the two wind turbines, one either side of the huge radio mast near North Pickenham.

Simply follow the stony track to reach the beautiful and peacefully sited church of Saint Mary at Houghton on the Hill which is well worth a visit. Carry on along the stony track which becomes a well

mown, wide grass path between hedges soon after you leave the church behind. At the end of the hedged section turn right onto a wide grass headland which is also well maintained and follow this round the field for some distance. Eventually the headland ends and you bear right to head towards a lane which is directly in front of you. There are houses either side at this point. Go straight down this lane until you reach a concrete loading area on your right in the dip.

NB The final section to the end of the walk follows a route which is an official footpath diversion and may be different to the route shown on your Ordnance Survey map.

Look for a small plank bridge over a drain on your left and take the narrow grass path uphill with another drain to your left. Simply follow this path, which is well used and very obvious as it skirts the field, making left and right turns a number of times round the corners of the field. After some distance, look for the footpath sign off to your left and go over another plank bridge. This path soon skirts the side of Ashill playing field on your left. About half way down the playing field edge the path turns right, makes a short crossing of a small field and then turns left. The path then follows the hedge on your right and goes between houses to reach Hale Road in Ashill with the green in front of you.

Did you know that ...

The name **Ashill** means 'hill of ashes'. It is an ancient community with evidence of Roman settlement in the area. In 1874 a gold torque was found there. Some house-holders have rights to keep a goose and a gander on the village green hence its name of goose green. Until the 1960s the village had a population of less than 500 but it has grown to its present size of around 1500 inhabitants today. The original school was replaced by a modern one in 1988.

Some parts of the **church of Saint Nicholas**, Ashill, are 700 years old and it is believed that it stands on the site of even earlier churches. The magnificent tower holds eight bells, six of which were original bells restored in 1996 when a further two were added. There is an unusual ogee-headed doorway on the west front. Inside the church, the font dates from around 1400 and contains carvings thought to represent Man, Woman, an Angel and the Devil. There is a memorial tablet to the eighteen men of Ashill who gave their lives in the Great War. The church is usually unlocked but if it is not, a notice in the porch indicates where the keyholders live.

The fascinating church of **Saint Mary the Virgin at Houghton-on-the-Hill** was a ruin until the late 1980s. Since then a local man, Bob Davey, has been the inspiration for its restoration. Bob is a retired engineer and he has transformed this tiny church and its peaceful setting into a beautiful building in a peaceful rural location. There is so much that can be said about this beautiful church which stands on the site of earlier churches going back to 630 AD. At that time the church would have been of timber construction. The stone church may have been started around 750/800 AD. Restoration, which started eleven years ago and which has led to the building being Grade 1 listed five years ago, has so far has cost over £100,000 and there is still much to be done.

For more information visit the excellent web site **www.saintmaryschurch.org.uk.** Sadly, though understandably given its remote location, the church is usually locked. However, arrangements for obtaining access and even a guided tour by Mr Davey are given on the church notice board.